WORLD SERIES CHAMPIONS

ST. LOUIS CARDINALS

Published by Creative Education
P.O. Box 227, Mankato, Minnesota 56002
Creative Education is an imprint of The Creative Company
www.thecreativecompany.us

Design and production by Blue Design
Printed in the United States of America

Photographs by Corbis (Bettmann), Getty Images (Bernstein Associates, Bruce Bennett Studios,
Diamond Images, Elsa, Focus on Sport, FPG, Otto Greule Jr. Hulton Archive, Paul Jasienski, MLB
Photos, National Baseball Hall of Fame Library/MLB Photos, Christian Petersen, Photo File,
Photo File/MLB Photos, Louis Requena/MLB Photos, Robert Riger, Mark Rucker/Transcendental
Graphics, Tony Tomsic/MLB Photos, Tim Umphrey, Ron Vesely/MLB Photos, Grey Villet//Time
Life Pictures)

Library of Congress Cataloging-in-Publication Data

Frisch, Aaron.
St. Louis Cardinals / by Aaron Frisch.
p. cm. — (World Series champions)
Includes index.
ISBN 978-1-58341-688-4
1. St. Louis Cardinals (Baseball team)—Juvenile literature. I. Title.

GV875.S74F75 2009
796.357'640977866—dc22   2007052465

First edition
9 8 7 6 5 4 3 2 1

Cover: Pitcher Adam Wainwright (top), shortstop Marty Marion (bottom)
Page 1: Outfielder Jim Edmonds
Page 3: Pitcher Jason Isringhausen

WORLD SERIES CHAMPIONS
ST. LOUIS CARDINALS

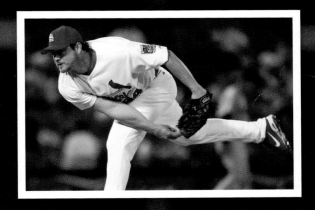

AARON FRISCH

CREATIVE EDUCATION

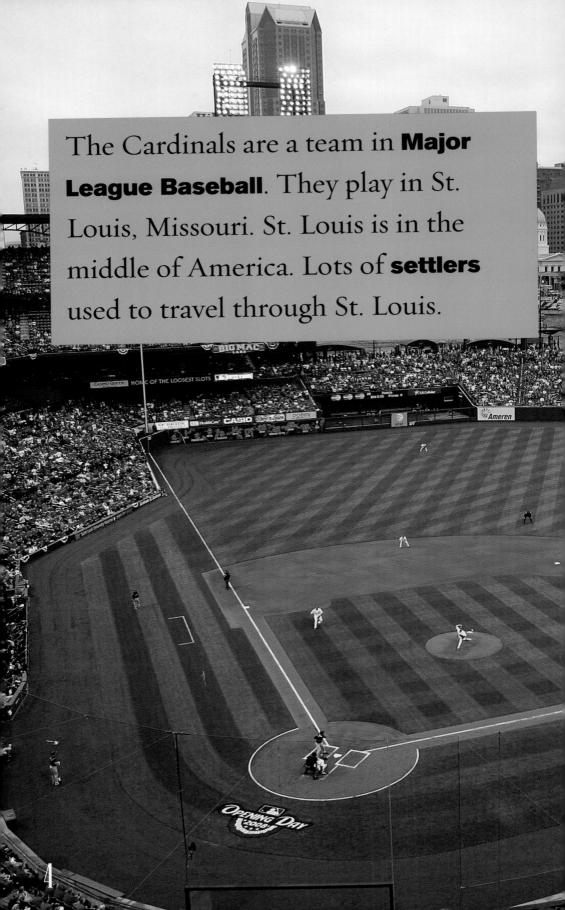

The Cardinals are a team in **Major League Baseball**. They play in St. Louis, Missouri. St. Louis is in the middle of America. Lots of **settlers** used to travel through St. Louis.

ALBERT PUJOLS

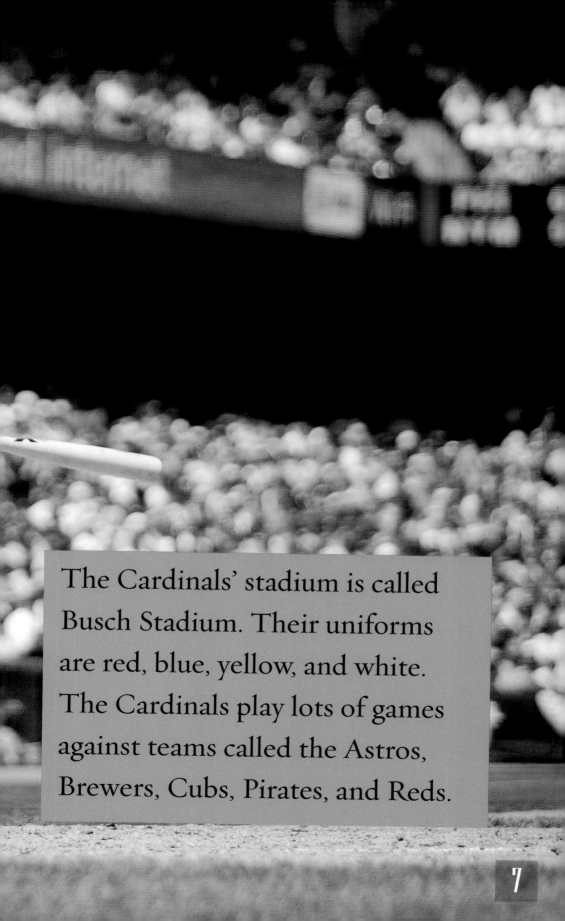

The Cardinals' stadium is called Busch Stadium. Their uniforms are red, blue, yellow, and white. The Cardinals play lots of games against teams called the Astros, Brewers, Cubs, Pirates, and Reds.

ROGERS HORNSBY

Outfielder Enos Slaughter

St. Louis's team started playing in 1882. Second baseman Rogers Hornsby was one of the best players. In 1926, the Cardinals won the World Series. They won it again in 1931.

Dizzy Dean was a good pitcher for
St. Louis in the 1930s. Dean and
his teammates liked to play jokes
and have fun. Fans called them the
"Gashouse Gang." They won the
World Series in 1934.

PITCHER
DIZZY DEAN

II

The Gashouse Gang

The Cardinals were world champions again in 1942, 1944, and 1946. Their best player then was outfielder Stan Musial (*MEW-zee-uhl*). He got lots of hits. Fans called him "Stan the Man."

OUTFIELDER
STAN MUSIAL

PITCHER
BOB GIBSON

Outfielder Lou Brock

The Cardinals were not as good again until they got some new players like outfielder Lou Brock. He was a fast runner who stole lots of bases. The Cardinals won the World Series in 1964 and 1967.

Outfielder Willie McGee

Shortstop Ozzie Smith helped make
the Cardinals a tough team again in
the 1980s. Smith was good at diving
to stop **ground balls**. He even did
backflips on the field before games!
He helped St. Louis win the World
Series in 1982.

ST. LOUIS CARDINALS

SHORTSTOP
OZZIE SMITH

19

First baseman Mark McGwire

St. Louis had more good players in the 1990s. First baseman Mark McGwire hit lots of home runs. But the Cardinals did not win the World Series again until 2006. Third baseman Scott Rolen helped St. Louis win that year.

THIRD BASEMAN

SCOTT ROLEN

21

FIRST BASEMAN
ALBERT PUJOLS

Pitcher Chris Carpenter

Albert Pujols (*POO-holes*) was another good Cardinals player. He played first base and was a big **slugger**. St. Louis fans hope that today's Cardinals will win the World Series again soon!

GLOSSARY

ground balls — plays where the batter hits the ball so it bounces along the ground

Major League Baseball — a group of 30 baseball teams that play against each other; major-league teams have the best players in the world

settlers — people who move into a new area to make homes and live there

slugger — a baseball player who is strong and can hit the ball hard

CARDINALS FACTS

Team colors: red, blue, yellow, and white

First home stadium: Sportsman's Park

Home stadium today: Busch Stadium

League/Division: National League, Central Division

First season: 1882

World Series championships: 1926, 1931, 1934, 1942, 1944, 1946, 1964, 1967, 1982, 2006

Team name: The Cardinals got their name because of their red socks. Cardinals are birds that are red. The team has been called the Cardinals since 1900. Before that, it was called the Browns. The Browns wore brown socks!

Major League Baseball Web site for kids:
http://www.mlb.com/mlb/kids/

INDEX